How to draw
Christmas

Fiona Watt

Designed and illustrated by Katrina Fearn,
Katie Lovell, Non Figg, Antonia Miller
and Jan McCafferty

Contents

Busy elves

Use the ideas shown here to draw a picture full of busy elves.

1. *Use a pencil to draw an oval for a head. Press very lightly as you draw.* Add a pointed ear and two little lines for the neck.

2. Draw a teardrop-shaped body. Add arms, then draw legs with tiny feet. Add a pointed hat, a frill around the neck and a skirt, too.

3. Either mix water with red paint and fill in the body, arms and hat, or fill them in with felt-tip pens. Fill in the skirt, legs and frill in green.

You could draw a shelf with lots of presents and toys.

4. Then, fill in the face and hands with watery paint or a felt-tip pen. Draw a circle on top of the hat and add some hair. Fill them in, too.

5. When the paint is dry, paint or draw rosy cheeks. Draw a present on the elf's hand and add ribbons and a big bow.

6. Use a thin brown felt-tip pen to draw over all the pencil lines. Add lines in her hair and looping lines on her skirt. Draw a belt, too.

Printed reindeer

1. Glue a piece of kitchen sponge cloth onto some thin cardboard. Draw shapes for a reindeer's body and head on the cardboard.

2. Use scissors to cut out both shapes. Then, spread some thick red paint on an old plate. Dip the body shape into the paint.

3. To print the body, press the sponge onto a piece of paper. Then, dip the head shape into the paint and print it next to the body.

4. Cut a strip of thick cardboard for the legs. Dip the edge of it into the paint, then print four legs at the bottom of the body.

5. Dip the cardboard into the paint again and print two lines on the head for the antlers. Print two shorter lines with a narrower strip.

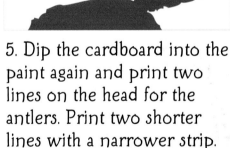

Twist the cardboard at one end as you print.

6. Print lots more short lines on the antlers and three lines for the tail. Then, print the ears, twisting the cardboard as you print.

7. Spread some light blue paint on the plate. Dip a fingertip into the paint, then print spots on the body and one on the nose.

You could draw spirals on the spots.

8. When the paint is dry, draw around the reindeer with a thin black felt-tip pen. Add dots for eyes, lines for hooves and add a mouth.

Starry sky

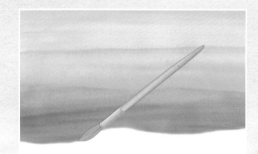

1. Mix lots of watery blue paint and brush it across a large piece of white paper. Make it darker at the bottom of the paper than at the top.

2. When the paint is dry, draw a faint line across the bottom of the paper, for a hill. Then, draw trees and buildings along it.

3. Draw an outline of a Santa and sleigh a little way above the buildings. Add a line of reindeer in front of the sleigh, too.

4. *Use black paint or ink to fill in the hill, buildings and trees, so that they make a solid black shape. Leave the paint or ink to dry.*

5. Then, fill in the Santa, reindeer and sleigh with a black felt-tip pen. Add a trail of tiny stars behind the sleigh with a silver pen.

6. Draw a moon and lots more stars in the sky with the silver pen. Then, draw rectangles on the buildings for windows.

Twinkly Christmas tree

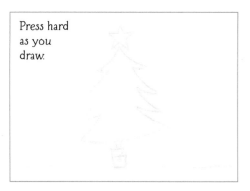

Press hard as you draw.

1. Draw a line for the floor across the bottom of a piece of white paper with a light green wax crayon. Draw a tree, its pot and a star.

The white crayon lines are shown in yellow so that you can see them.

2. Draw some presents beneath the tree. Then, use a white wax crayon to draw stars around the tree and add spots on it, too.

3. Mix lots of watery yellow paint, then brush it all over the paper. The wax crayon lines and shapes will resist the paint. Leave it to dry.

Paint some orange presents, too.

4. Brush watery pink paint over the tree, presents and floor. While it is still wet, dot yellow and orange paint on the tree. Fill in the star, too.

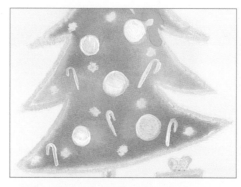

5. When the paint is dry, draw large round decorations and candy canes with thick white paint or correction fluid.

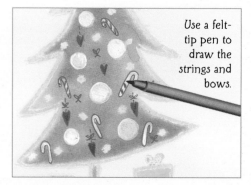

Use a felt-tip pen to draw the strings and bows.

6. Draw hearts on the tree with a red pencil. Then, add strings and bows to some of the decorations. Draw stripes on the candy canes, too.

7. Spread white glue on the big white decorations and sprinkle them with glitter. Put dots of glue on the star and sprinkle it with glitter, too.

8. Draw around the glittery decorations with a bright pink pencil. Add a shape at the top for hanging and fill it in with a paler pink pencil.

9. To make the tree twinkly, blob little dots of glue onto the tree. Then, press a sparkly sequin or bead onto each blob of glue.

This tree had gold
paint added
around the star.

Jolly Santas

For a scene like this, paint the sky blue and finger paint blobs of white snow.

This Santa's sack was finger painted with dark brown paint.

You could draw a dog wearing a Santa hat.

1. *Use a pencil to draw a circle for a head and another one for the body. Then, draw curved lines for the arms and legs.*

2. Dip your finger into some thick red paint, then finger paint a hat on top of the head. Finger paint the body, arms and legs, too.

Overlap the prints for the boots.

3. Finger paint brown blobs on the end of each arm, for mittens. Then, do two overlapping fingerprints for each boot.

These reindeer were painted, then lines were added with a pencil. for fur.

4. Mix some paint for the face, then finger paint the face and ears. When the paint is dry, print a darker nose and slightly paler cheeks.

5. Unravel a cotton ball. Pull off little pieces for the cuffs, and pieces for the hat and the bottom of the jacket. Then, glue them all on.

6. Tear a long beard from the cotton ball and two smaller pieces for whiskers. Glue them on, then draw the eyes with a black felt-tip pen.

You could draw a line of footprints in the snow.

Snowy skaters

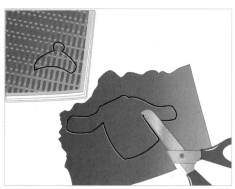

1. Rip different pictures of clothes from old magazines. Use a pencil to draw a sweater and a hat on the pictures, then cut them out.

Add the ear halfway down.

2. Glue the sweater onto a large piece of white paper. Draw an oval head above it with a blue felt-tip pen, then add the eyes.

3. Draw a mouth and some hair and fill them in. Draw mittens at the end of each sleeve with a paler pen. Then, draw a skirt and fill it in, too.

Add some birds and animals with a pale blue felt-tip pen.

This dog's scarf was cut from paper and its body was drawn with a pen.

4. Draw two curved legs and add feet. Fill in the legs and feet. Then, draw two short lines and a curved blade for each ice skate.

5. Glue the hat on the top of the head. Then, draw several more skaters in the same way, using ideas from the picture above.

6. Draw a little fence around the skaters for the edge of the pond. Draw curved lines for tracks on the ice. Then, add trees behind the pond.

Three Wise Men

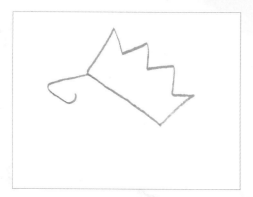

1. Use a pencil to draw a crown at a slight angle, near the top of a piece of white paper. Then, add a curved line for a nose.

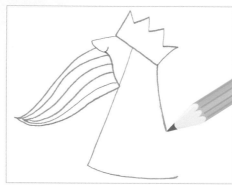

2. Draw a beard joining onto the nose and add some curved lines inside it. Then, draw a headdress hanging down from the crown.

3. Draw a long shape for the body. Then, add a cloak, flowing out to the side. Draw two pointed slippers below the body, too.

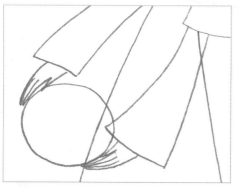

4. Draw two sleeves. Then, add curved shapes for hands. Draw a circle for the gift between the hands. Erase any lines that overlap.

5. Mix paint for the skin and fill in the face and hands. Add red cheeks. Then, fill in all the clothes with different shades of watery paint.

6. When the paint is dry, draw over all the pencil lines with a thin black felt-tip pen. Add an eye, and the lines in the beard.

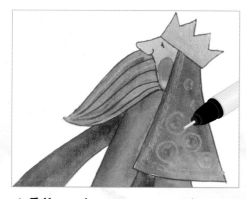

7. Fill in the crown with a gold felt-tip pen. Add some gold lines in the beard, too. Decorate the headdress with lines, dots and circles.

Fill in the top part of the gift, too.

8. Draw gold stripes along the bottom of the body and on the sleeves. Decorate the rest of the body with lots of little dots and circles.

9. Draw a patterned border along two edges of the cloak. Then, draw lots of lines down the cloak, following the flowing shape.

In this picture,
the Wise Men
were drawn first,
then the sand and
sky were painted
around them.

15

You could decorate a stocking with patterned circles, instead of lines.

Christmas stockings

Use a gold or silver pen, too.

1. Paint lots of stripes with different paints, across a piece of white paper. Do some thick ones and some thinner ones.

2. When the paint is dry, use felt-tip pens to draw spots, stripes and other patterns on some of the thicker lines.

3. Draw a stocking on the paper and cut it out. Draw around it on plain paper. Cut out shapes for the top, heel and toe, and glue them on.

16

Icy snowman

Draw the head about halfway down your paper.

1. Draw a circle with white chalk on blue paper for the head and fill it in. Draw a larger circle below it. Add a wavy line and fill in below it.

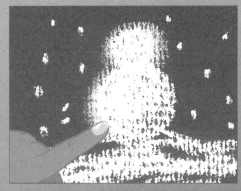

2. Draw chalk dots around the snowman. Rub the edge of the snowman with your fingertip to smudge the chalk. Smudge the dots, too.

3. Lay some scrap paper over the bottom of the picture so you don't smudge it any more. Draw black pencil dots for eyes, a mouth and buttons.

4. Draw a nose shaped like a carrot and a scarf around the neck with a bright red pencil. Then, fill them in with red and orange stripes.

Make your scene more magical by adding a Santa and reindeer in the sky.

Try drawing a church, like the one above.

Snowy hill

1. Draw a curve for a hill on a piece of dark blue paper. Fill it in with white paint. Then, draw stars in the sky with a white pencil or chalk.

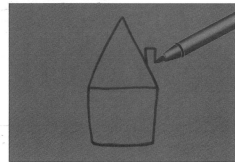

2. For a house, draw a square with a dark pink felt-tip pen on a piece of pink or purple paper. Add a pointed roof and a chimney.

Make one of the windows round.

3. Draw some windows and a door on the house. Then, add crossed lines inside each window, and a handle on the door.

4. Draw rows of U-shapes for tiles on the roof. Then, fill in the tiles with a white pencil, making sure you don't go over any felt-tip pen lines.

5. Fill in the wall of the house with a lilac pencil. Make the windows orange and blue, and the door red. Fill in the chimney with lilac.

6. Draw a large triangle for a Christmas tree with a dark pink felt-tip pen. Add a small trunk at the bottom of the tree, like this.

7. Draw three zigzag lines across the tree to look like branches. Then, draw a star at the top of the tree and fill it in with an orange pencil.

8. Fill in the top of the tree with a white pencil, then use different shades of blue and green pencils to fill in lower branches.

9. Draw several more houses and trees in the same way. Then, cut them out. Arrange them on the snowy hill, then glue them on.

Angels with sparkly wings

You could draw one of
these angels on the front
of a Christmas card.

1. *Use a pink pencil to draw
a circle for a head. Add the
neck and shoulders. Then,
draw the outline of a dress
with long sleeves.*

Draw little circles on
the cheeks with a
red pastel, then
smudge them.

2. Fill in the face, neck and
shoulders with a chalk pastel
or a pencil. Then, draw
hands and legs – they don't
have to be very neat.

3. *Use a black pencil to draw
two curved lines for eyes
and eyelashes. Add a smiling
mouth. Then, draw little
wings beside her shoulders.*

The cloud in this scene was drawn with orange, pink, red and white chalk pastels. The pastels were then smudged with a cotton ball.

4. Fill in the top of the dress and the sleeves with a yellow pastel. Then, fill in the rest in white and smudge the pastels together a little.

5. Add wavy lines with red and yellow pastels for frills on the dress. Draw a red and yellow halo above the head and add little red shoes.

6. Draw some hair with a red pastel and smudge it a little with your finger. Then, add some curly lines to the hair with an orange pastel.

7. Spread glue onto the wings and sprinkle them with glitter. Leave the glue to dry, then shake off any excess glitter.

Fun in the snow

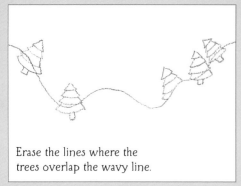

Erase the lines where the trees overlap the wavy line.

1. Draw a long wavy line for the hills, across a piece of white paper. Then, draw some triangular-shaped trees along the line, like this.

2. For a girl pulling a toboggan, draw a circle for a head. Add the body, arms and hands. Then, draw the legs and feet, like this.

3. Draw a hat. Then, add some hair. Draw her eyes, nose and mouth, too. Then, add a line around her neck for a scarf.

4. Draw a toboggan beside her foot. Add a curve along the front edge, too. Then, draw lines joining the toboggan to her hand.

5. Decorate her clothes with stripes, and add pockets and buttons to the coat. Draw a seat and footrests on the toboggan.

6. Fill in the girl and the toboggan with lots of different felt-tip pens. Then, draw over all the outlines with a thin black pen.

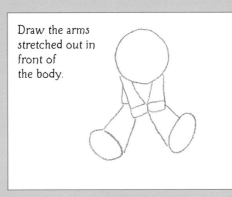

Draw the arms stretched out in front of the body.

7. For someone sitting on a toboggan, draw the head and add the arms. Then, draw the body and legs, and ovals for the feet.

8. Draw a rectangle for the toboggan around the body. Then, draw lines across it, and one for the front edge. Add curved runners, too.

9. Draw a hat, then add ears, and hair flowing out on each side of the head. Add eyes, a nose and a mouth, then fill in the drawing.

Leave parts of the trees white, for snow.

Draw footprints and tracks in the snow with a light blue felt-tip pen.

Festive trees

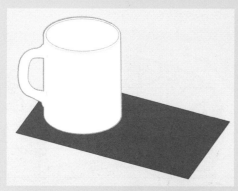

1. Place a mug or a cup near one end of a long rectangle of dark paper. Draw around the mug with a pencil, pressing lightly.

2. Draw a trunk and a plant pot below the circle. Then, draw a large bow with flowing ends, a little way down the trunk.

3. Use a light blue pencil to draw a small holly leaf in the middle of the circle. Then, draw more holly leaves around it and fill them in.

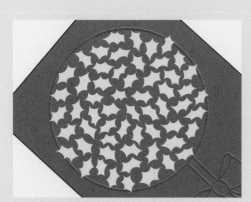

4. Continue drawing little holly leaves at different angles until you reach the edge of the circle that you drew in step 1.

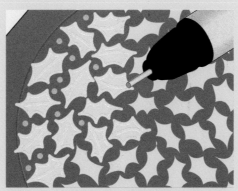

5. Draw around each leaf with a silver or gold felt-tip pen and add some little dots for berries in the spaces between some of the leaves.

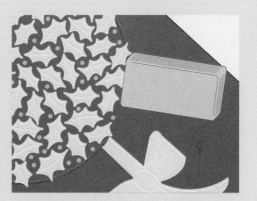

6. Outline the trunk, the bow and the plant pot with a gold or silver pen. Then, carefully erase the pencil circle when the ink is dry.

You could draw a snow palace in the background.

Ice queen

Draw the face near the top of your paper.

1. Draw a heart shape for the face. Add a curved eyebrow. with the nose joining onto it, then draw the other eyebrow. Add lines and dots for eyes.

2. Draw a mouth, then add lines for ears. Draw a crown above the face and add wavy lines around it for the hair. Add lines in the hair, too.

Draw curls on the end of the sleeves.

3. Draw a neck and add a curved collar. Draw the arms and add hands with pointed fingers. Add sleeves, and a cloak billowing behind her.

4. Draw a long body and a flowing skirt with swirling curls at the bottom. Then, go over all the pencil lines with a blue pencil.

The lines are shown here in yellow so that you can see them.

5. Draw more curls on the dress with a white wax crayon. Draw lines in the hair and cloak, and add some coming from the fingers.

6. Paint clean water all over the paper to make it damp. Then, blob turquoise ink or watery paint onto the paper around the queen.

7. Then, brush very watery paint or ink onto the body while the paper is still damp. Paint darker dots and swirls too. Then, let the paint dry.

Sparkling decorations

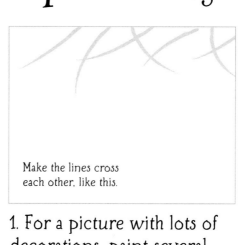

Make the lines cross each other, like this.

1. For a picture with lots of decorations, paint several curved lines for branches along the top of a piece of paper, with silver paint.

2. Paint lots of shorter, thinner lines along each side of the branches. Leave the paint to dry while you make the decorations.

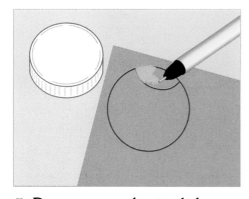

3. Draw around a jar lid or a roll of tape on a piece of pink paper. Draw a curved line inside the circle and fill it in with a gold pen.

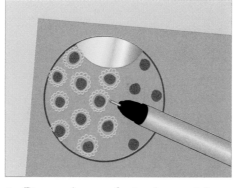

4. Draw lots of circles with a red felt-tip pen and fill them in. Then, draw a line around each circle with a silver pen and add little petal shapes.

5. Cut out the circle and glue it below one of the branches. Then, use a toothpick or an old match to dot white glue onto each red circle.

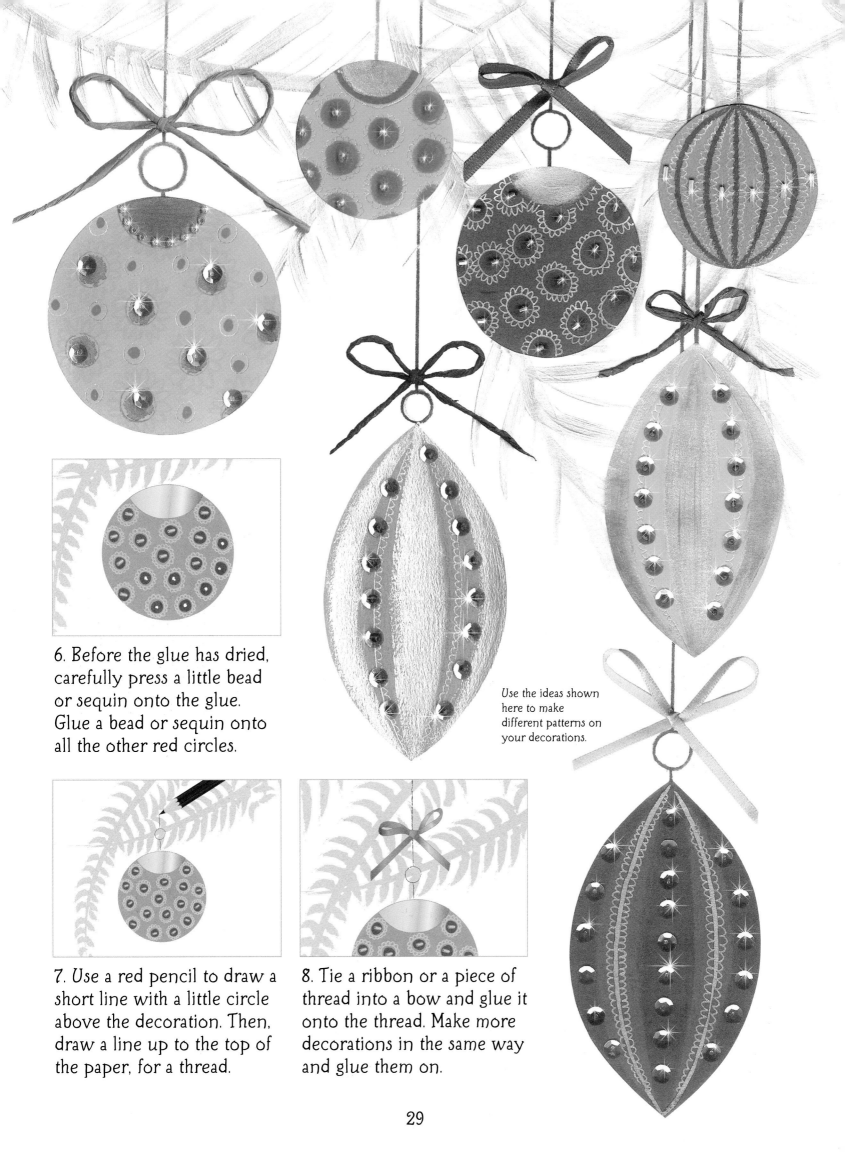

6. Before the glue has dried, carefully press a little bead or sequin onto the glue. Glue a bead or sequin onto all the other red circles.

Use the ideas shown here to make different patterns on your decorations.

7. *Use a red pencil to draw a short line with a little circle above the decoration. Then, draw a line up to the top of the paper, for a thread.*

8. *Tie a ribbon or a piece of thread into a bow and glue it onto the thread. Make more decorations in the same way and glue them on.*

Trees in winter

1. Draw a tree trunk with a blue felt-tip pen on a piece of paper. Then, add branches coming from the trunk. Add little twigs on the branches.

Draw the tree trunks bending at different angles.

2. Draw lots more trees in the same way. Draw large ones at the bottom of the paper and much smaller ones at the top.

Make the zigzags a triangular shape.

3. Draw green zigzag trees in between the other trees. Draw a short line for a trunk at the bottom. Fill in any spaces with purple trees.

4. Add dots for snow across the paper with a white wax crayon – they are shown here in yellow so that you can see them.

5. Draw some hills above the trees with a pencil. Then, mix some watery blue paint. Fill in the hills and paint a shadow beneath each tree.

6. When the hills are dry, mix some darker blue paint and brush it across the sky. Then, leave the painting to dry completely.

7. Dip a clean paintbrush into some water, then brush it around and around on top of one of the trees. The ink will run in the water.

8. Brush water over all the other blue trees. Then, brush water over the green and purple trees, rinsing your brush each time.

31

Snowflake patterns

Use the ideas shown here to draw patterns of your own.

1. *Use a pale blue pencil to draw four lines that cross each other in the middle. Then, draw four more lines with a blue ballpoint pen.*

2. Draw a circle in the middle with the pen and fill it in. Then, add a circle to the end of each line with the blue pencil.

3. Draw small leaf-shaped patterns along all of the pencil lines. You'll find it easier if you turn your paper as you draw them.

Photographic manipulation by Nick Wakeford and John Russell
First published in 2005 by Usborne Publishing Ltd., 83-85 Saffron Hill, London, EC1N 8RT, England www.usborne.com